Life Lessons from

ALSO BY CHRIS KRESKI

GROWING UP BRADY
(with Barry Williams)

STAR TREK MEMORIES

STAR TREK MOVIE MEMORIES
(with William Shatner)

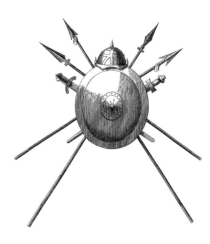

Life Lessons from

XENA
WARRIOR PRINCESS

A Guide to
Happiness, Success, and
Body Armor

CHRIS KRESKI

Andrews McMeel
Publishing

Kansas City

FOR AMELIA ROSE KRESKI,
Warrior Third Grader

www.andrewsmcmeel.com

98 99 00 01 02 RDC 10 9 8 7 6 5 4 3 2 1

Library of Congress Cataloging-in-Publication Data

Kreski, Chris, 1962–
Life lessons from Xena, warrior princess : a guide to happiness, success, and body armor / Chris Kreski.
p. cm.
ISBN: 0-8362-6767-2 (pbk.)
1. Success—Psychological aspects. I. Title.
BF637.S8K74 1998
158—dc21 98-13635
CIP

Design and composition by Mauna Eichner

ATTENTION: SCHOOLS AND BUSINESSES

Andrews McMeel books are available at quantity discounts with bulk purchase for educational, business, or sales promotional use. For information, please write to: Special Sales Department, Andrews McMeel Publishing, 4520 Main Street, Kansas City, Missouri 64111.

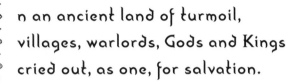

In an ancient land of turmoil,
villages, warlords, Gods and Kings
cried out, as one, for salvation.

Only one warrior could
answer their prayers.

I am Xena.
I am Warrior Princess.
My secrets may guide you—
in business, pleasure, and love.
I am here to help.
READ ON!

Leadership is an intangible quality. Leadership has no all-encompassing definition. Leadership becomes self-evident only through action, experience, satisfaction, and example— or a corner office.

oo often, life asks the true leader this question: Conquer or run away?

A Warrior Princess never runs away.

Instead, she fights, she battles, and in the rare instance where she knows in her heart that she will lose...she delegates.

opper breastplates
intimidate.

Thigh-high boots
convey power.

Weapons are always
appropriate accessories.

Dress codes are not to
be taken lightly.

n successfully presenting new ideas to allies, it is important to use clear, concise language and powerfully persuasive arguments.

Should there remain opposition toward any of your initiatives, a boot to the head usually presents an effective alternative solution.

peak softly,
but carry a
big stick...
and a sabre, and a
knife, and a singing
sword, and a mace, and
a shield, and a lasso,
and a killer Frisbee,
and...

Never
put
off
until
tomorrow—
what
you
can
decapitate
today.

emember:

Gazing toward the heavens
for divine guidance may be
good for the soul, but it
also leaves you vulnerable
to the attacks of surly
midgets.

emember:

Never practice your smiting
on an ally. Blood spilled
unnecessarily can never be
erased from the mind's
eye...nor can it be easily
removed from living-room
carpets.

CONSIDER:

> Callisto is evil personified.

> Callisto is a sociopath.

> Callisto fancies herself a leader...
> bitterly lusting after the power held
> by her superiors, while twistedly
> plotting their collective doom.

CONCLUSION:

> Callisto is NOT a leader.

> Callisto is middle management.

ith a smile, a positive attitude, and a cheerful disposition...you can get up really close to an enemy and kill him before he has ANY idea what the hell's happening.

Success

is

99 percent

perspiration...

and

1 percent

avoidance

of

the

bubonic

plague.

ood grooming is essential to success. All warriors should consider being bathed and deloused on a quarterly basis.

eechings are
considered
an elective
procedure and as such
are NOT covered under
existing medical plans.

successful minion keeps up with the cutting edge of technology. In today's Knownworld, being abacus-literate is a MUST.

As always, habitual tardiness, unacceptable productivity, and the disemboweling of coworkers are all grounds for immediate termination.

Always be politically correct. Centaurs now prefer the term "equine-Knownworlders" to the previously accepted "big-fat-hairy-assed-stupid-smelly-half-horse-guys."

ending a brief thank-you note to a fellow warlord, after you've enjoyed a successful summit meeting, is considered good etiquette.

Sending a sympathy card to his next of kin, after you've killed him, is also encouraged.

omance within the ranks is frowned upon. However, extraordinarily close, wildly flirtatious, sexually ambiguous friendships between Warrior Princesses and their nubile, young, strawberry-blonde companions are, as always, highly encouraged.

t's true, beauty really is only skin deep. I mean, once you've gouged through that first inch or two...trust me on this one.

emember:

Should you be kidnapped, bound, and teased by Callisto or any other beautiful, curvaceous, though thoroughly sociopathic, supervillain, please bring it to my attention immediately... and in vivid detail.

otivation of troops can be accomplished through praise, clear communication of the task at hand, and powerful speech. Or, you can just skip all that, and let loose with a well-screamed "YIYIYIYIYIYIYI!"

riumph requires only simple tools: honor, logic, and of course an arsenal of swords, daggers, maces, lances, rocks, sticks, and the occasional dead eel.

ourage is born of the heart.

Leadership, of the soul.

Victory, of the left knee... applied fiercely and repeatedly to enemy testicles.

THE DOUBLE STANDARD

When the male warrior expresses a strong, clear, aggressively defended opinion, he's considered a forceful speaker.

When the female warrior kills that male for HAVING that opinion, she's considered a bitch.

pportunity must ALWAYS present itself equally to warriors of both sexes—in that the only career choices actually REQUIRING a penis or vagina are, in all likelihood, illegal.

t has been stated that the quickest way to a warrior's heart is through his stomach: This is a fallacy.

The quickest way to a man's heart is to hack in, forcefully, just above the solar plexus.

With practice, the entire process can take less than twelve seconds.

any feel that Callisto suffers from multiple psychoses.

I do not.

I believe she thoroughly enjoys each and every one.

onventional wisdom states that all of the best men are either married or gay—one ponders whether it might be a fair assumption to believe this statement might apply to women as well.

COMPASSION

The successful male
warrior makes a carefully
constructed first
impression. He presents
himself forcefully,
overflowing with bravado,
brandishing sword and
sinew in a well-oiled,
gleaming display of raw
power; flexing every
sweaty, blood-engorged
muscle in an orgy of
machismo, intimidation,
and self-confidence.

The successful FEMALE warrior witnesses such displays with a reserved, restrained visage: laughing out loud only AFTER said warrior moves out of earshot. Anything less would simply be cruel.

he female warrior seeks in her mate the qualities she herself holds dear: wisdom, compassion, humor, intelligence.

The male warrior seeks in his mate a heart of gold...preferably buried beneath a bosom that defies every known law of physiology and gravity.

The warrior's shield protects her from the slings and arrows of distant enemies. Her wristlets protect her from the blades and spears of hand-to-hand combat. Her black leather miniskirt, geometrically constructed, protects her from the hippiness of a slightly meaty behind.

JUSTICE

An eye
for an
eye,
a tooth
for a
tooth,
a broken neck
for a
broken heart.

It is believed that Zeus created man long before woman. With that in mind, one may contemplate and better understand his initial creation as a sort of first rough draft.

he sharpest and most devastating weapon of the Warrior Princess is not forged of steel, but merely of flesh. It is her tongue, and with this solitary, diminutive muscle she can swiftly, almost effortlessly, slice apart any male enemy.

Quick, unexpected cuts to the ego have proven particularly effective.

male warriors often put this princess in the mind of Argo. Both species are malodorous, temperamental, and hairy, but on occasion, they can provide an enjoyable ride.

ale warriors routinely lose their temper, display anger, and openly and enthusiastically seek to destroy their enemies; their actions are not only accepted, but expected.

Were I to awaken one morning as a male, I would no longer exist as an anomaly, an exception, an aberration...I'd simply be normal.

Of course, were I to awaken one morning as a male, I'd probably fling myself off the top of Mount Olympus, but that's beside the point.

ven a Warrior Princess must consider the feelings of others. Brief expressions of common courtesy can make her every adventure far more pleasant—a simple "Good morning," a sincere "Thank you," a well-placed "I'm sorry, was that your spleen?"

As Warrior Princess, one must break free from the vicious circle of negativity and leadership through fear. Instead, she must foster an atmosphere of safety and trust. Allies who fear that substandard performance will result in their being skewered may suffer in their work...thus increasing their chances of said kabobbing.

n leading large armies, the effective Warrior Princess must always be aware of ever-changing financial considerations. Pension plans, for example, now tend to drain available capital, as it's no longer unheard of for retired warriors to survive well into their early thirties.

If at
first
you
don't
succeed...
can
I have
your
stuff?

hen angered, do not allow yourself to merely lash out in rage.

When that happens, you've let your opponent get the better of you.

Instead, take a deep, cleansing breath and count to X, XX, perhaps even C. When you've composed yourself, you can rationally and calmly disembowel any antagonist without allowing animosity to muddy your exchange.

Warrior Princess cannot allow personal comfort to put collective safety at risk. An afternoon nap may be good for the soul, but it can be hellish on life expectancy.

emember:

If you are unhappy with your current situation, the best time to look for a new position is BEFORE you've run through your current employer.

Encourage underlings to continually set goals for themselves and revise their own job descriptions. For example, Gabrielle has successfully implemented her own vow of mastering the weaponry techniques of her fighting staff. In future months we're hoping she'll be as successful with some of the goals I'VE assigned her. They include a vow not to yammer incessantly, a vow not to screw up every single assignment I ask of her, and a vow not to bear any more children of the devil.

PHRASES THE TRULY SUCCESSFUL WARRIOR PRINCESS SHOULD RETIRE IMMEDIATELY

✠ "Oh, I'm pretty sure those villagers can take care of themselves."

✠ "Joxer, can you help me with this?"

✠ "Hey Salmoneus, how about a song?"

✠ "Autolycus, while I'm fighting this battalion of Huns, could you hold my purse?"

✠ "All right, Callisto, but this is your last chance."

And of course:

✠ "Hey Gabrielle, tell me all about your day."

NEGOTIATION

The art of negotiation can be tricky. It involves flexibility and a friendly, delicately rendered verbal give and take—right up until the moment you squeeze your adversary's neck at the appropriate pressure points and repeat the following: "I'VE JUST CUT OFF THE FLOW OF BLOOD TO YOUR BRAIN. IF YOU DON'T TELL ME WHAT I WANT TO HEAR, YOU'LL BE DEAD IN THIRTY SECONDS. FEELING CHATTY?"

The Xena Pinch—honest, straightforward, highly effective.

allisto leads through fear. She relishes the opportunity to interrogate through torture, and she screams with delight as she skewers the helpless. Relentlessly, she attempts to destroy my soul and tear apart everything I hold dear....There is, it would seem, a very fine line between passion and just being a total asshole.

This Warrior Princess must never again get carried away with her own individual assaults upon the ladders of victory, fame, conquest, and fortune. Remember, placing yourself on a pedestal above your allies accomplishes nothing...except maybe to give them a really clear view of your black leather underpants.

epeatedly, I have been impaled with arrows, bumped, bruised, contused, sliced, diced, twisted, cracked, smacked, squashed, squooshed, clobbered, scraped, and bitten; yet I've emerged victorious and smiling, time and time again. I am the living proof of the ancient axiom that when you win the fight, nothing hurts.

CONSIDER:

Gabrielle is beautiful.

Gabrielle is almost entirely incompetent.

Gabrielle's latest performance review was unbelievably positive.

CONCLUSION:

Gabrielle continues to require my close, personal, hands-on supervision.

no one is guaranteed victory—not even this Warrior Princess. Some days, despite your very best efforts, the fire-breathing dragon is going to win the battle. On such occasions, the truly successful leader does not wallow in defeat. Instead, the mere avoidance of flame-broiling should be considered a victory.

The Warrior Princess must be dedicated, but she must also remember to leave her work AT work. Bringing home hordes of hapless villagers, widows, and orphans in need of protection can be a bit stressful, and hellish in the outhouse.

UNIVERSAL CREDO

Believe in yourself, seek out new challenges, and you WILL succeed–unless you're Gabrielle, in which case believing in yourself and seeking new challenges will only result in you getting into deep, DEEP trouble and screwing up my life immeasurably.

arrior Princess can be an exhausting career, and for that reason, one must always be sensitive to the early warning signs of burnout. These include: irritability, loss of appetite, boredom, and of course, lots and lots of dead guys all over the place.

e flexible
and
creative;
there's more than one
way to skin a giant
one-eyed flying
cyclops.

e aware and sensitive to sudden behavioral changes and mood swings in your allies. Increased absenteeism, fatigue, and lack of focus can all be early warning signs of grog abuse.

emember:

Should you be ambushed by several dozen bloodthirsty gladiators, cry out for help immediately. It is selfish and greedy to kill them all yourself.

ecause I am a Warrior PRINCESS one might expect that I'd believe strongly in the equality of the sexes.

I do not.

I have no intention of stepping down from my position of superiority.

SYNERGY

The process of two or more warriors working together, combining their unique personal skills toward a common goal.

Example: Gabrielle and I were once kidnapped, held captive by a giant, drooling, flying, cannibal cylops. Separately, we would have been doomed. However, as Gabrielle employed her storytelling abilities to bore the behemoth into a near coma, I was able to make ready my concealed bosom-hidden dagger-launcher.

As Gabrielle continued her incessant jabbering and the monster's eyelids drooped, my décolletage let fly with a well-aimed direct hit to the forehead. We were free seconds later.

rief periods of meditation can be deeply relaxing and reenergizing to the busy Warrior Princess. The process simply requires a peaceful, stress-free environment, complete silence, and of course the absence of Gabrielle.

INTERPERSONAL PROBLEM-SOLVING STRATAGEM FOR THE 1190s B.C.

Step One—In a comprehensive, concise manner, study the situation at hand, as well as the feelings and underlying motivations of the malcontent.

Step Two—Carefully evaluate both sides of the disagreement, taking careful measure to remain nonadversarial, open-minded, and just.

Step Three—Repeatedly beat the malcontent over the head with the nearest large, heavy, blunt object.

Step Four—Repeat Step Three.

RECIPE FOR SUCCESS

Step One: Build one enormous rotisserie.

Step Two: Build one enormous bonfire.

Step Three: Purchase 762 gallons of barbeque sauce.

Step Four: Battle gigantic mutant wild boar.

Never underestimate the power of positive thinking.

Each Warrior Princess should proudly display her own style, her own personality, her individuality. No one can be exactly like Xena. Most days I have a hard time doing it myself.

hould the Warrior Princess find herself momentarily intimidated by an especially formidable opponent, one effective method of regaining composure to simply imagine your enemy almost entirely naked and performing the legendary "dance of the three veils."

Time and again, this simple exercise has worked very well for me, even in confrontations

with Hercules. It's amazing
how much less threatening a
muscle-bound foe can appear
in mid-wiggle.

Strangely enough, I'm told
that even to this day,
Hercules often imagines
ME nearly naked and
performing the dance of the
three veils as well.... I'm
flattered. I had no idea I
was that intimidating.

hy is it that the male soldiers who will fight and die beside me to ensure that all men remain free find not the slightest drop of irony in looking forward to the day when they'll finally go home—to be reunited with the women who will spend the rest of their lives cooking for them, cleaning for them, sleeping with them, and slavishly catering to their every whim?

abrielle, on a regular, almost daily basis, makes my life more chaotic, more difficult, more headachey, more EARachey—but she also makes it more colorful, more vibrant, and a lot more fun. That is why I NEVER consider leaving her.... I consider MURDERING her about twice a day, but leaving her, never.

hy is it that in a world crammed with warlords, soldiers, kings, and Huns, 99 percent of the time I have the biggest balls in the hut?

he life of a
Warrior Princess
is not an easy one.
It bears the pain of battles
lost, the sadness of fallen
allies, the incredible
chafing of a gigantic metal
wonderbra.

One should always take careful steps to ensure that the solution to any given problem doesn't cause more of a problem than the original problem. The handkerchief can be every bit as effective as the sabre-in dealing with a persistent runny nose.

abrielle has studied the works of the truly great writers; she has learned their axioms, memorized their truisms, and can quote prodigiously their most profound thoughts. Why is it then that, whenever she agrees with one of my decisions, I immediately experience the uneasy butterflies of impending disaster?

he bigger they are, the harder they fall—which is important to remember lest an enormous enemy cyclops collapse upon your head.

As a last resort, should brilliance, strength, wit, and charisma all fail, bullshit may provide a worthwhile alternative.*

✳ A chakram to the Adam's apple works well too.

am not a well-schooled woman. Instead, I have learned my lessons from experience, mistakes, and the heat of battle. If ever there was a shining alumnus from the school of hard knocks, it is I. My diploma can be found, printed in black and blue, at points of varying interest from head to toe.

ades has been crowded of late with formerly "omnipotent" warlords, all of whom perished from a common affliction. It's called "refusing to consider negotiation as an alternative to battle with 'any mere female, even if she is a Warrior Princess.'"

PHRASES THE SUCCESSFUL/SURVIVING MALE WARRIOR SHOULD RETIRE IMMEDIATELY

✠ "Warrior Princess Shmarrior Princess, no woman tells ME what to do."

✠ "Xena, you're such a bitch today. What are you, like, on your period or something?"

✠ "You know what they say about guys with long swords...."

✠ "Bet you even STAB like a girl."

✠ Well why don't YOU just leave the seat UP?

✠ No, I WON'T stop flipping through
   channels with the remote.

✠ "Wow, Xena, did you get fat or what?"

✠ "Why no, I'm NOT wearing a cup.
   Why do you ask?"

And don't forget:

✠ "Hey, Gabrielle, tell me all about
   your day!"

here has been quite a bit of con-
fusion and debate regarding the
sex of my palomino, Argo—but I
really don't think it would be fair for me to
provide the definitive answer. I believe
that sex is a very personal matter, and for
that reason I will simply state that Argo
is whatever your own intuition dictates.

However, feel free to read
whatever you wish into the not-so-
subtle subtext the horse knowingly,
winkingly, and continually provides.

I f you love something, set it free. If it returns, it is yours forever.... If it doesn't, it's probably just gotten into yet another screwy predicament that will force you to go out and save its ass yet again, after which it won't be at all thankful, prattling on incessantly about how it wasn't HER fault she got her pretty little red head into trouble and that she'd have been just fine on her own and really didn't need you to save her in the first place and.... Sorry.

Callisto is an unshakable and increasingly annoying affliction. She is treatable, beatable, and defeatable, but just when you think she's finally gone for good...she's back, with a vengeance, driving you even crazier than before. She is a yeast infection in thigh-high boots.

A well-screamed "YIYIYIYIYI," a well-thrown crescent kick, a well-flipped chakram—all of these will do more for the soul than any silly little book of pseudo-clever advice ever could.*

 *Of course this information is best understood only AFTER purchasing said "silly little book of pseudo-clever advice."

To those of you who find Gabrielle irritating, I will confess similar feelings on occasion. However, I would also remind you that, according to Homer, it is the constant irritation of the sand that allows the oyster to rise above its less than spectacular nature to create beauty, magic, the miracle of the pearl....

All right, it's a stretch, but it keeps me from smacking her...most of the time.

You can't win them all, but in the Warrior Princessing industry, your first loss immediately changes your job title from "hero" to the much less desirable "decapitated martyr."

ld chakrams may lose their effectiveness, but they're damn near impossible to throw away.

e are told from birth that the gods atop Mount Olympus are omnipotent. Why then, in my experience, do they need ME to haul THEIR big, fat, all-knowing asses out of a sling every single week?

he more experienced I get, the more confused I become. Each new dilemma I encounter seems to provide a moral quandary that demands ever-increasing amounts of soul searching. No decision comes in black and white anymore. I suppose that's because I am just no longer young enough, brazen enough, naive enough, capricious enough, nor stupid enough to believe I have all the answers.

t is true that from time to time Gabrielle has been known to rub me the wrong way; however (I'm sorry, this one's just TOO easy-please feel free to supply your own dumb punchline here).

TOUGHEST ENEMIES

I have emerged victorius in legendary battles with Callisto, the Bacchae, even Goliath—but many even tougher battles were fought without fanfare, documentation, or a publicist. A list of my most fearsome enemies follows.

Gingivitis

Reesus Peesus

Dr. Zaius

Ficus Benjamina

Janet Reno

Enuresis

Jimbackus

Apostrophes

Elephantiasis

Attila the Jehovah's Witness

Chlamydia

Wacko Jacko

Grilled Chicken Caesar

Alexander the Incontinent

Menses

Hairybackus

Bob's Big Boy

And of course—The Thighmaster

INEQUALITY

I will never comprehend the phenomenon wherein the accumulation of power somehow manages to erase the male warrior's faults. Power elevates an ugly warrior to "ruggedly good looking," makes a fat warrior "barrel-chested," a stupid warrior "unpretentious," an ancient warrior "mature," a

poorly bathed warrior "musky." Power remains a highly effective aphrodisiac—the best friend of hideous, flabby, dumb, old, smelly warriors who'd stand NO chance of getting lucky without it.

Somehow, if I should be lucky enough to wind up old, gray, wrinkled, and a bit more than pleasingly plump, I find it hard to believe the reverse will be true.

f a Warrior Princess can keep her head about her while those all around her are losing theirs, she probably has REALLY good aim with her battle-ax.

ool me once, shame on you. Fool me twice, shame on ME. I mean, breaking each of your fingers, then your toes, then stripping you, painting you purple, gluing a bouquet of large ostrich feathers to your ass, and hanging you, upside down, off the roof of the public library...well, that may have been a TAD excessive.

ever look a gift horse in the mouth—unless of course said horse is fifty feet tall, made of wood, and has been rolled into your city by a battalion of Greek soldiers.

anners and civility
are assets to any
Warrior Princess,
except on the battlefield,
where wild-eyed, screaming,
howling, eye-gouging,
fingernail-raking,
testicle-twisting,
ass-kicking, premenstrual,
banshee-bitchdom
serves her much more
effectively.

t has been my experience that no plan of action can ever be deemed foolproof—especially when Joxer is involved.

unny how the smaller, weaker, profusely bleeding side of any altercation is generally first to acknowledge the errors of his ways.

hould the day arrive wherein ALL of your strengths and talents ultimately fail you on the battlefield—should you find yourself flat on your back, an enemy gloating down at you, blade at your chest—fear not...you can easily survive even this. Simply take one deep, cleansing breath and watch closely as your evil superfoe prepares to run you through. He will surely:

A. laugh maniacally to the heavens,

B. tell you in GREAT detail how his evil scheme will play out once you've been eliminated,

C. spout a really lame one-liner at your expense, i.e., "DID YOU HEAR ABOUT TODAY'S SPECIAL ON WARRIOR PRINCESSES? THAT'S RIGHT, ME AND MY BATTLE-AX ARE ABOUT TAKE 50 PERCENT OFF!"

or

D. all of the above.

For some reason, ALL murderous evildoers indulge in these behaviors before smiting their victims—and their momentary lack of focus provides a nice little opportunity for you to pound them into a wriggling weeping puddle of gelatinous goo. Works every time.

Conversely, in the heat of battle, the effective Warrior Princess should ALWAYS take time to say something cute just after knocking out and/or running through any soldier dumb enough to get in her way—something along the lines of:

"Nighty-night, don't let the vultures bite."

"I'm sorry, was that your nose? Or are you eating exceptionally rare meat loaf?"

"Wow, you really DID have a lot of guts."

"Look, a Hun-sicle."

Be clever. Be original. Use your imagination. It's a small courtesy, but victims have come to expect it, and like mints on a pillow or complimentary mutton, it's the little things that separate the mediocre from the truly great.

When
in
doubt,
knock
him
out.

tudy everything and everybody: I learn much from the sage advice of Salmoneus, but even more from Joxer's endless series of screwups, poor choices, and bad examples.

eal happiness comes not on the battlefield, not in conquest, but in finding a companion loyal enough, brave enough, smart enough, and loving enough to make your heart lighter. It doubles in knowing that you're fully qualified to return the favor.

very Warrior Princess
knows that her most noble
conflict rages perpetually
within the boundaries of her own soul.
With every breath, every fiber of
muscle, and every bit of resolve, she
must constantly struggle to overcome
her past, to make better her present,
and to strive tirelessly toward a more
admirable tomorrow.

Battle forever!

no gods, goddesses, bards, centaurs, cyclopses, Amazons, bloodsucking Bacchae, kings of thieves, warlords, soldiers, green egg men, demon babies, jumbo-sized cocktail rats, oversized Polynesian-style bamboo horses, frock tarts, banshees, incredibly coincidental identical twins, winged harpies, dryads, slippery eels, publishers, editors, proofreaders, typesetters, or bookstore clerks were harmed during the production of this handbook.

However, it should be noted that this Warrior Princess is indeed experiencing some of the early warning signs of carpal tunnel syndrome.